GOOD STOCK
STRANGE
BLOOD

GOOD STOCK STRANGE BLOOD

Dawn Lundy Martin

COFFEE HOUSE PRESS
Minneapolis
2017

Coffee House Press books are available to the trade through our primary distributor, Consortium Book Sales & Distribution, cbsd.com or (800) 283-3572. For personal orders, catalogs, or other information, write to info@coffeehousepress.org.

Coffee House Press is a nonprofit literary publishing house. Support from private foundations, corporate giving programs, government programs, and generous individuals helps make the publication of our books possible. We gratefully acknowledge their support in detail in the back of this book.

LIBRARY OF CONGRESS CATALOGING-IN-PUBLICATION DATA

Names: Martin, Dawn Lundy, author.
Title: Good stock strange blood / Dawn Lundy Martin.
Description: Minneapolis : Coffee House Press, 2017.
Identifiers: LCCN 2016057020 | ISBN 9781566894715 (paperback)
Subjects: | BISAC: POETRY / American / African American.
Classification: LCC PS3613.A7779 A6 2017 | DDC 811/.6—dc23
LC record available at https://lccn.loc.gov/2016057020

Images found throughout the book are stills from the film *Good Stock on the Dimension Floor: An Opera* by the Yam Collective, directed by Sienna Shields. All stills are courtesy of Sienna Shields, except on page 54, courtesy of Tamara Weber.

PRINTED IN THE UNITED STATES OF AMERICA

24 23 22 21 20 19 18 17   1 2 3 4 5 6 7 8

Contents

GOOD STOCK STRANGE BLOOD

Prologue

Q: *If your book is a house, what does the foyer look like?*

The book is a like a long, thin, wavy tendril stretched into the sky from a small spot at the top of my head. At the end of the tendril, somewhere far in the sky where I cannot see, is a mutilated black face. A little me is sitting on the top of my head, holding the tendril like the string to a balloon.

Q: *Whose blood?*

The blood is a corrupt(ed) document of one's fate. But when I am beautiful, and young, and open, with no features that distort or take away from, it's easy for the stranger to enter the space of the body like a god. Does the blood become a further stain on wet, light feet? I dunno. A psychic once told me that I would live a very long life— epic, she said, like in a Russian novel. Really, it's only blood. Very symbolic. So many days I spend in bed, bleeding out of my vagina, so hungry I'm distorted. I call people to my bed until I feel depleted enough to sleep.

Q: *We are wondering why there is a small self. Maybe the prologue is your body.*

Because the question at the center of the book is, *Why doesn't one just die?* And the little me is holding the thin line because there is a squashedness to existing in the present and I can't think about—

Q: *What I like is that the little self is holding the tendril like a balloon because it gives me the impression that you are letting this mutilated thing go.*

—I can't think about how to exist now without pressing together big pasts and small pasts. Big pasts (like historical collective trauma) and the narrow self-indulgent past of personal invasion, self-configuration at the hands of another. The mutation of blood. The development of the multiple. Anyway, the little one holds the weight of the past. Maybe she's already dead as she sits. Who knows? But then, as I was writing this book, it was the summer of Sandra Bland and then the summer of Freddie Gray, and then some cute kid was shot in a big-box store while holding a toy gun, and so many other of these deaths, unexplained in the logics of the rationality we hold so dear. And the white boys are hand-slapped for brutal rapes. Life just goes on. The past isn't the past but the present. It's all laid out in the same space / time plane; the tendril becomes like a reaching into another dimension. Its symbolism changes.

Q: *Why exhale after the inhale? The breathing is the mantra. Could the trauma be keeping us alive?*

What happens is: we walk through a door. On the other side of the door is a manifested future place. It's configured very differently from this one. Its shape is different. But we created it so we recognize it; we understand its workings, which are mostly based on intuition. In the book, what's keeping us alive is the ability to imagine something very other than what's been shoved down our throats, what's been taken up in our cells. To imagine something other is to leave the known world. No death. But, instead, the door. To place a body alongside the grubby stranger, and then the stranger in a lockbox, and then voilà: a self is three intentional selves. And, the three selves are like different manifestations of the thing we call "blackness."[1]

---

1. Some of the poems in this collection have been reconceptualized from their original context in the libretto *Good Stock on the Dimension Floor*, written for the HOWDOYOUSAYYAMINAFRICAN? global artists collective (the Yam Collective). The video installation piece of the same title, directed by the Yam Collective's Sienna Shields, premiered on Opening Nights at the Whitney Museum's Biennial Exhibition in 2015 but was withdrawn by the collective, in protest of the museum's racist and sexist curatorial practices, before the exhibition opened to the public.

Conceptually, the libretto was organized as follows:

The characters are no longer named in the poems that appear in this book, a gesture that takes its lead from the Yam Collective's interpretation of the text. In the text's enactment, multiple people inhabited and portrayed each body.

CAST:

LAND	The black embodied body
PERPETUUS	Reflection of LAND
NAVE	Plural

NAVE has been born from the head of Sarah, the protagonist in Adrienne Kennedy's one-act play *Funnyhouse of a Negro*; she is continually peeling off her skin, only to find another layer beneath it. When Sarah, who is haunted and fractured by the blackness of her father, apparently (maybe) hangs herself at the end of Kennedy's play, NAVE [I imagine] emerges in human form but with many arches and windows. She sings the problems of existence on earth. She sings from a deep memory and historical torment. NAVE is both haunted and empowered by connectedness to ancestors and traditions.

LAND is symbolic of the way the body can be trapped by racialized existence. LAND exists in a perpetual state of longing, enclosure, and toil. (It should be noted that LAND's utterances do not find their way into this book.)

PERPETUUS, LAND's primary reflection, exists in a sphere of other kinds of knowing the black body. PERPETUUS is untethered from the history of the body on Earth. S/he can weep without melancholy. S/he can sing through dimensions, through universes, and is unconnected to any sense of linear time. Though her/his skin is brown, s/he is without race boundary as s/he is without gender boundary.

Throughout the narrative, LAND becomes more and more grief stricken until, at the end, speech is impossible. LAND resorts instead to moans, grunts, and muffled cries. These sounds cannot be written.

PERPETUUS begins to transform into LAND instead of being mere reflection.

To Shed the Traces of Catastrophe . . . ?

Aglow, this bent

      body. Itch of layer, knot of
hair—they call us *Negro*.

To stand broad-footed in sensation of being lit up.

No monument,
      only blood-earth,

warm salve to open throat-bone.

How to live between Mother and time?

As if born into the self watching
      the self, already made, formless, then out of clay.

Feel the hump of our drape. Here: the body, flesh
      inevitable, unsatiated hunger like a whip—

Instrumental fissure, instrumental fish, whose rasp
      a whip, a book, a story left in the dark body,
to reach fingers out toward shine of morning, eyes squinted,
and find there only cordgrass, some smoke or a warning.

- - -

He said, *If they would only just beat or shoot me, but they wanted soul substance, to harbor that like that, so I could never move from this place. They reach crackled hands inside and hold me open for raking.*

Our name . . .

What is our name?
Where are the buttons holding
us in place?
What is place outside of time?

Outside of memory—un-stitched,
un-snatch, swell into—

Our mother's "blackened" skin,
her "tarnished" "whiteness."
Her rope shackled to grandfather's
black neck—

A picket, a thicket, rice, cotton,
sugar, potatoes, cowpeas,
turnips, and rye—O, lord, thank you
for Mr. Hopeton not selling my boy.

This is the body bending over another.

Textures, we know them—

        bruises, our Missus's homespun cape,
linen hung by its lips, sway
—a useless body,
        trash boy.

What is a dance for being?

A step toward nothingness.

Grey, landscape, purple feet,
        I remember, I swear,
the limp relative to nothing.

Scraps, bright against sea,
        migrant legs almost
drowned already, a narrative

        wired in cells, desolate root.

We succumbed—

     head by measure, by—

weight of black sheath and organs,
     legacy that lingers
     —a hip thrust.

We wait in wings,
     expanse spread across
     darkening blue sky.

     We shut shades—
     huff into wings, shrink

     bones of self.

     What you drag:

     your banjo, your braided
          neck-lace. Disappearance

     into mole. Stink of flesh become flesh.

Come now—

     arms and arches open
to pocket all dejected souls—

- - -

—in play or games, or anticipation. What it means to live almost primarily in this space, to escape the ordinary state of anxiety. What allows the body to survive, to maintain an unpunctured exterior? What is wholeness if we were never whole?

- - -

O, release, this rough
        rot—

to be born of Sarah's head, through
        sieve, seized wreckage,

our laboring hulk—age-old sag—

Scarf-wrapped faces.

        Quarry

                metal dust   beyond dark space

        is possible   tribe

        under stain, father's black tongue—

—Neck exposed toward sky

shins bubbling in heat—

positioned losses, one in each archway

picturesque as summer—

a layer gone, another absolute without—

the robberies—

Ibibio shrine. Ibibio man in a cowboy hat.

What's a condition and what's a duration. As in, so far I've remembered one dream in the past four months. Two bright moons, one a reflection of the other, but I couldn't tell which was which.

—The holding place—

on edge of continent—late day falls—gut
tumbling, night warm, welted warmth [We

      bracket infinity]

Stare through this window in

      my belly where Mother

left her good stock, her pertinent cells,

      her matter that matters—

Tiny particles forever floating—

"What is more frightening than a black face
confronting your gaze from the display case?"

—My form against those at border—

[arbitrary line] [perish]

    knocking among other refugees

      —the islands
      —no one to help
      —thousands buried by water

A butchered animal at my feet.

Wolves howl. Soot falls from sky.

The rescuers are never prepared.
And we, here, amid a failure of images.

Scrub a spot whiter than before.
Demarcate before there is nothing left.

Breath into white sand. The dead ache so.

The Baby Book

—To be in covering

     is the problem, hunger caverns
under this leather wrap—from destitution—
from split skull—

     Mother as brown as—
brawn and braided,
       toward—filth beneath,
       skin like wire—

     all our kin.

From before—
     —It happened when—
dust under foot, red dick stuck,
under guise of reason.

Who summons us
       from darkness,
from water well, one philtrum
       stitched to Wolof tongue—

Who tugs and rocks us, suckles wet mouth? We is the purpose of the
falling, swollen, our teeth hurt, their constant cutting. Warm when
sunken. Wanted the swell of black earth, a legacy, *something larger
than ourselves to hold us.*

If I were looking from the outside—

I'd think that a thing ancient would not pulse so loudly, would be automatically removed from the atmosphere, lose its atomic structure, its relatability. We were driven. Or we were rode hard. Mule-like on feathers. This notion of sustainability: black vultures everywhere, neat white stars under wings, good at cleaning up road carcasses. What a mess mess, your weak veins, your lifelong addictions. What you then must witness is the vulture devouring the exposed red and fly soaked—   unrecognizable.

—The book

      of repression—

all the stuff brilliantly cocking my throat
no dream remembered
      no past reconstructed

he called it a kiss but that was no kiss

—rises, dead breath into smoke
the writing is not balm
the *I* in sleep is unreachable,
subtle flesh, skin warm milk, salt marsh
—its simplicity. Without warning.

– – –

In my early thirties I had one recurring dream so vivid it began to feel like a memory rather than a dream. It's the only dream worth recounting. At some point, I no longer held the dream, just the memory of the dream told, and often I'd get confused as to the nature of non-dreamed life. In a giant old abandoned house at the top of a hill, it's night and I am furtively burying a man's body under some floorboards. I pull up the floorboards and then I'm outside digging a grave with my hands. It's easy, this digging, and I know there will be no evidence of this activity. I'm free to carve out soil in big rough scoops. Even though I know I won't get caught my body is wracked with guilt. But I cannot stop; the burial is necessary and compelled so I scrape the earth, bludgeon it with bloody fingers, and then place his body into the shallow grave, replacing the floorboards. No one will ever know.

– – –

Elision
into vowels
sunken time
O sounds, *OU*
short flat *a*
for as long as—

My brother bends away from the hose that beats him. Basement is a watery place. I think of privacy and houses, what they allow for, their intimacy of enclosure. *We never heard a word from over there and they never heard a word from us.* How the home seals off the world, creates a hole in the world, and there is no joy in that. To watch a teenaged boy compressed and the heart still beats, is hiss, is what hatred made. God will not save you.

—A last leaf

undercover.

Three days in bed.

You think, hurry and
get to the real black bits or no one will care.
You have no sage advice,
you are no magic black, there's no head
to rub. I play a game.
I'm living
a normal life
in utter aloneness
fossil of aloneness.

When I slice off a chunk of my finger
with the sharpest knife,
wonder if anyone in town
will be up for a fuck
the book is not writing itself
in the chilled gray day.

Here's a mirror to show you your ghost self and how it feels the same to be weighted by a body as it does to have the body become transparent.

Imagine a beautiful fracture, a wondrous contortion, a backbreaking arc. It will do the body in. No way to hold that kind of thing.

Mother, at 83—

labor or resurrection—

is stunned to find out that people remember their dreams. *Occasionally*—she says—*not vividly.* I tell her, *me too.* But we are not like many other people.

I want to provide a metaphor for darkness.

I want to tell you that the other day, while writing this very book, I became piercingly depressed as if a bird had crashed into the window, and when I'm depressed I want to feel worse because that can be a comfort—my brick feet, my open casket with the hole in my chest exposed so you can see right through the body, the glossy wood, through the floor and then to layers of earth, catacombs and rites of passage.

I searched for the man who notched the hole (could not remember the spelling of the name in my mouth so many times).

Shiny perpendicular—my cunt wet all day—
        legions of waste in my body

Desecration—
Defunct—
A symphony

I took a photograph of him, this man, and realized it was not me in the casket at all, but him. I stuff gauze into the wicker box that has become "life source." Fluent gnaw. *O, this is where I keep him tucked,* I say to myself, *this is where he lives.*

His obituary is perfectly respectable. What is this dead language?

No one

    will admit the facts of the matter even though logbooks provide the material. They look at the gloves and say, *gloves.* That's it. And you are hoisted up on stretcher, paraded through crowded streets. Contortion of hacked body.

Greengrass
greengrass
greengrass
greengrass

grows

Only *I* see my stranger.

To split
to be spilled
to topple
to be topped
to strain
be stained
strangled.

Robe falls open—
against my belly—
stroked.

- - -

Whatever disintegrates does so in a fashion that can hardly be recognized. The constraints of the book are limiting. We must always consider the bigger book of grief. What I could not know, what no one can ever know is how laden an effect is predicated on an event or a progression of events.

- - -

Black stars fill up black sky—

a dark stairwell up two flights to shag rug. I will lie here for a long while. I will be unspectacular and limp. When the opal stone appears, I'll lean into it. But terror is a runaway train. Is deer head left on side of road, those gentle deer eyes staring softly at nothing. If the stone works at all, it's easy to catapult my body up the gymnasium rope knot by knot—a willowy thing, until relief under billowing fragrance of the parachute, all our little forms cross-legged in wonder. When I stand now at the edge of the earth, night close and tight around me, no difference between what was undreamed and what happened. For example, my stranger ever-beckoning, black eyed and grinning, or is it me who dislodges packed dirt from the hole the earth made?

Symptomatic of being a slave is to forget you're a slave, to participate in industry as a critical piece in its motor. At night you fall off the wagon because it's like falling into your self.

—fetish object—

deploy sensory mechanism

deploy sound canon

blow their fucking eardrums out

shoot them at close range if you can

rationale of the uninterrogated actual

in the side yard bright wind takes sprinkler's sprinkles up into sunlight

I call for my stranger, I long for him. I look for him in the face of every black ghost on the edge of every piss-stinking park. Can taste Bacardi breath, the long tow of it, lapping against skin, pressure in what can't happen and does. An imprint: how the slender living room window looks out onto the street, a sofa perpendicular to window in front of TV. The kitchen table—Formica—my feet dangling. Or was that the motel that one time—who allows—who doesn't say, *wait*, into a room of bicycles where the children fetch their toys. A thing you don't want can make you ravenous, can open the sturdiest lip with its faint presence.

The proposition that compels the book

is already flawed, hovering somewhere between memory and fantasy, repetition and desperation. I know how you'll cock your head. You ask, "What is memory?" But what I mean is that any existence inside of both loss and abundance feels impossible. You can't have your cake and eat it too. Don't rob Peter to pay Paul. Somehow, after all these years I'm still alive. I cannot stand to exist against the banal. I'd rather be a monster than live inside of your cereal box. And I was a monster, wasn't I? Did I grin when you suffered? An estimation of justice. That night in question, how an infection entered my pussy and got hold. Like you, I am unforgiving. It might be a perversion of my blood, inherited like a sore. What language my grandmother spoke, I cannot tell you. On the census records from 1903, the word "laborer." My mother is crippled, and I will live in her place, a stain in the hegemony.

The Black Bits

"sometimes just bottoming out facing the dull ugly
fact of a violence / violation"—Maggie Nelson

The Negro in the Desert

Cattle land, I've never
        seen it, even in sleep,
break up the two-lane.
        Over there, he says,
        that's Juarez,
        just past the river.
"What goes ape in the night
        is a nigger with a fly
on his toe." Ever hear that one?

"That dirty N-
and his toes"
nobody thinking about
but I have seen them,
chaotic from labor,
the father's feet
got another foot
attached to them
got a leash around
their foot necks,
damn black stumps
and all over newspaper
he cuts 'em
and we run out
laughing cause
there's no foot like that
ever, black sentinel
knives, goddamn
this fortress undesired
because what desire
could live here?

I got another one,
        because why end there?
"Them old nigga fingers look
        like Slim Jims."

Tobacco Shade

"She had been made half with real white blood."—*Gertrude Stein*

Or.
She been made
real with half
white blood.
In keeping
with tradition
sun blackening
continued, shoe
got nothing
on the field hand.
If there is a theme
it invades,
under our tongues
like poison seeds,
and we forget
our names.

Our Wandering

We in a shit
      rustle, the way
in ramble and camaraderie,
brown hand of whose mother
makes its smooth noise
      over my mouth?

The burden of saying
      some *thing*, a head-
nodding, and I want to be in-
side of your knowing. Who
      lays their head
      on the disappeared's pillow?

      One minute a person licks your ear,
      the next, you cannot see your own white breath.

We gotta head
      on over to the party way
out in Bushwick because we're lost,

and our flesh is on fire. There's
a man walking behind us. And growing.

This is what I tell him:

      I am not a boy in anyone's body.

      I am not a black in a black body.
      I will not kowtow inside your opposites.

How the world blisters you.
How hunger left you statued.

– – – – – – – – –

One falls past the lip of some black unknown, where time, they say, ends.

We got us a sugar-
      mouth, a bit feeding,
walk in circles in circular rooms
built so precisely for our shapes,
      hold the figure that is the body that is,
of course, me.

I stroke the feather that feeds me,
that lines my cage floor with minor luxuries,

I say "ma" into its wanting sugary mouth.

What is the difference between ash and coal,
between dark and darkened, between love
and addiction on Dekalb at 2 a.m., and I fall
drunk from a ruinous taxi, already ruined
from *before* before, the absent weight screams
into your breath, *you are no good, no good* . . .

The space between *I* and *It*. Lolling.

The Ibibio man was not born in his cowboy hat.
Even *his* throat must ache like tired teeth.

The whites are calling themselves Border Police.

To be an orphan inside of "blackness"

—is the condition of it (us). We can love it, sure, cradle its beautiful head, and eyes looking. It wants to be performed, leaping, but the *I* is not a good actor. The problem of the book is that it's never quite "black" enough. Language can perspire the thickest blackest blood but you are still the unheld nigger, the one inspiring the deadly shaking panicked rage. Your tennis shorts or salmon-colored pants will not help you. It's a good idea to have "black" in the title of the "black" book in case there are any questions as to its race. The "black" bits will be excisable, quotable in reviews. The book should be very interested in the thing you know as "blackness," all its clothes, its haberdashery. What the book actually wants, however, is to know the distance between the "I" and the "you," how it is drawn into space and action as when the white woman professor says you have written her a "vicious" letter and wants to know what's wrong with you. Claudia Rankine has reinvented this territory of the relation that is forever unrecognized in that relaxed [white] body. When one's actions have so clearly produced the interrogative text, the refusal to enter the text as subject. For you, the text lives in the floating unreal, a document that has nothing to do with you, but, my dear, it *is* you, the grotesque monument to the regime, so perfectly sculpted you cannot see yourself in the mirror.

Obituary

Plastic gaze into plastic coffin,
no calling up the wet stare
the wet mouth
contorts into lie,
I love you like a saw
into barely beating
heart, my body hard
and flat against the coffee table
as dry blood,
urgent wheeze
girl splayed life anchor
but this is not what
the obituary says.
It says, *beloved husband,* says
survived by, condolences,
not, *there were others.*

No Humans Involved

When I was a girl of 9 or 10
anyone could have me
any way they wanted
because speech
closed a blackness
in my throat
so cavernous and loud
the blackness,
a smoke so thick
don't even think about
the procession on the body
all their maws loaded up.

Done found

the well

where the girl died / her body just tangled, you know / they liked to call it strange fruit / the stench and witch of our synchronicity / and how we burden / foreclose the claim / with wells and things / and police / and citizens / and accidents / no one / no one will ever really know the already known / the surface of the earth sometimes just opens up and says gulp / you, too, could be the body dismembered / sometimes only one other person knows the mechanics of the incidents compelled like desire / like I want to fuck slash kill you / like my dog chases and froths at his mouth / hey, play me a song I'm so hungry /

The Other Baby Book

The interrogative open turf   seconds before killing

Layer bodies on top of other bodies   Precise for destruction

Heaving . . .   Breath gasps in sweat

Spit and blood and shit (Undoubtedly)   Blood pools

Joy interruption in blood   The size of a body dropped in curve

Cradle of any head   We cannot imagine it

Curve as in queer   As in a path run off

No thought of it yet there it is   Fault lines huge movement

Out of the woods to lay waste   Savage containment

The door is ajar   Then abruptly not

– – –

Maybe god says, Let's let this one come to being in service
to this other one's imploded need. *This is what remains in
my body now that my stranger is dead. When do we become
the book?*

– – –

Dear Stranger,

I know how you lie in my mouth to my mother, how you wrap yourself up in juicy presents and other tokens of your appreciation. I know how you stir at night dreaming of a body you can hold in your palm, however briefly before the monsoons. There were dead girls, too. Do you remember? Or, a dead girl behind the corner candy store. Only scant record of her in the dusty archives of the local library.

*Symptomatic of being alive
is the arm stretched out into
starless air.*

*When the genealogy is cut
either by will or demonstra-
tion, there's not an easy way
to retrieve or go back to. What
exists in the place of what's
unavailable to you?*

When this is a nonspeaking—

when it can crack already sidewalked, the small square of it, because you too are a hand reached up from soil, and it formulates, a shape of O, tongue respondent, wordless frame that gestures and in its movement, resonance around it, it's okay to want a claim in the thing. Everyone is talking around you. You are—hem me a cliché for god's sake—where is she? You know, the stuff around the thing that's not so hard—

Father in dead logs—

My father eating a plate of boiled okra,
false teeth rungs clackin'—
Him drinking a plate of beers
Him large and dim
on crackling skins
or fat from pickled pigs
Him saving me from choking on an ice cube,
picking too many strawberries with me in a field
slunk down drunk in the back seat of the Buick
Me driving steadily
the road almost on fire
with no eyes
My father glowing under white gazes,
shining like a fucking flaccid ninja
Them rocky parents in the front seat
Them cussing their barely cusswords
Them working on all fours all the time
Time passes like a dragon; cosmos winking at us
According to blanched root, to flagrant history,
Come round and up, invisible, with bright teeth.

—I could tell you how to fall—from one sphere to another. You see, you fall through the gut and when you arrive at the next place, you squeeze a rough hard knee. You keep pushing the stranger out because you do not want to see him. What other place is possible besides your stranger? A smell so sweet it makes you vomit? A slippery blue cot that aches in your head like ice? Your nose bleeding giant clumps of blood down your throat for no apparent reason? Some slices of orange on a tray rejected? You want cookies. You want to lose yourself in confection.

Want touch   ***want devotion***

      Unfolded—
          lose grip—

      ~~Our mother was queen~~
         ~~of all of Europe!~~

      Mother, this is our head
         on a tendril root
      waving into sky—

         Lift last leaf of skin,
      place inside a doorway—

Discovery of ineptitude: I will never be able to give you what you want.

You want to open palms up. You discover dark punctures. You discover black bleeding nails.

When you leave the compound, you discover a larger compound. You're traveling in the wrong direction.

—A list—

Two swing sets—one for the little kids, one for the big.
A skinny man who teaches you how to play chess.
He is the good one.
Heart drops swing, a girl's body wound 'round the horizontal pole.

Some snapshots.
A gaze away.
We leapt, didn't we?
What a regular thing.
We soaked out dirt and blood from clothes.
We placed them on a big rugged rock, sat in the sand, and waited.

Swallowed red bone. Some kid painted it, grew in lush green, stood out like a welt. An adult white couple—a man and a woman—befriended us, wanted to discover something. We sat on the boat, went clamming at a cold shore. It was the thing to do. But we were vigilant in protection; nothing, no crowbar could force open the seal or solvent. This is historical subject—blue collar black, the way of impermeable breach, no one's cool swaddle to secure the body, waves of flesh—the darkness comes in any lake house.

Things will simply appear—rotund and circular, a gigantic berry left for anyone to experience. Freshwater streams, lakes: for drinking. I position my chest against any smooth surface. I roll around in any fat heart. To suck the wreck, jaw unhinged from vessel, cavity spotted in white pocks. *You have to let go,* says the voice, *just let it happen, it's how pleasure comes.* If the voice comes from my stranger, then a whisper of debris blows past my ear.

We Believe in Regarding the Nature of Being

The Rinse.
    Because a—

    branch bent in a V toward sun / whereas legitimacy of this witness / ing / Lacan's first, core loss and the recognition of one's self / my head into lamb's breath / black breath could be a noticing of marking or slashing / how am I gonna be your dog if you keep asking me questions? / I could just crawl around with my tongue hanging out. would you like that? / in Kindergarten a girl called me / ******* / a smell of doctoring / witch hazel on a girl's face / all souls are lost, I know this / if I crawled on the floor might feel like home / grate upon jagged grate / can you feel that? / as if were lung stone / when we say breathing or / air /

Winter—

to trace

a life is to trace nothing at all but accumulation of events which them-
selves are not things / *Mother, where are you?* / what questions burn
the edges of your heart? / I see the wrought iron cage you've spent so
many years carving / careful attention to one's own insignificance in
God's hands / God's little bird / pale day / crest over walk into leaves
Mother in her house of leaks / roof tumble / in haze of light / shackle
light / what in the world is this missing? / what exists in the deep ways
of broken things? /

—untethered from happenings rooted to temporality—

The *I* is made of many arches and windows. Enter this structure, the entrances to the many houses of god.

And yet, each morning a fireheart grief coming out of sleep. The listening to the smoke as if fills and weeps inside the chest, choking strength out, hands weighted, dangling. We wonder where else it lives before it fills us up. We assume it comes inside through the hole that promises invasion.

—This layering of forms pushes you toward abstraction.

—We have stolen madness from the white people.

—An Asian white man will call us a *crazy bitch* in a text.

But we have long done been free. Coffee is brought to our bedside on a silver tray. We are unrepresentable. We sip into the griefmouth.

We're all just little humans.

As if from a dream, as if without form.

They said

there are rules to attend to and washing and wearing of the jumpsuit, which is the color of the walls in my childhood room.

The owl in our mouths cannot say *oust* or *out*.

The crying elephant. The crying elephant.

The boy says, "I was completely depleted of vitamin D and drank Purell Hand Sanitizer and instant Kool Aid just to feel something."

The way of Athena, her wolves at her feet.

You roll over—
     catch

     your persistent umph. The minutia of a hello. The old people don't like it but we like it because we live there as our selves enacting imprint selfhood.

The record of our worst things. To heave into a hole too small for you.

How the promise is destroyed. *God is dead. Life goes on.* All the small things like dust. The big things like starving.

I'm going to tell you now of the smallest flower. It's called *Wolffia globosa* or *watermeal,* and it's green. It floats on the water in clusters—you've seen it—but if you have a problem looking at certain textures, you might get sick looking up close. It's edible, especially in Asia.

The Book of Love

And in likeness, foreignness or incompatibility. Which strain darkens the hair?

If one could be giddy with dif-
ference, this is it.

In this visioning everything is slowed down to recognizable speed. A seduction in minu-tiae. Tangential becomes a kind of center.

Seer said, betrayal is always a symbol of the soul being upgraded.

Unintelligible whisper calls me a long way.

Big big, *I say*, bigger.

Perpetual underneath, even when subtexts are revealed, stuff buried in other stuff.

We've come a long way, baby. Your extraordinary promise, sweet excessive force.

A want to know which name when.

High Priestess reveals something the I *has never seen before. Hidden document not briny or waxen, smells of soft sand.*

He found more than a text, he found a whole life, some years of it, and they are calling it material.

Restraint, form, some per-missions. I want to say, "cunt" here, "cunt ache."

Subliminal fury as in housemaids.

What it means to shed dry urge, wicker. Was horse-hair wad. Was restaging. Every movement forecast, exact, rendition in abandoned amusement park, the ground damp behind dead carousel damp.

Or forests or company. Or other unchecked situations. As a result, some heretofore unknown architecture in place of our weapons of security?

All expertise slips off the ledge.

Deception is often a reciprocal activity.

When desire is not produced by what you don't have.

What it must be like wearing a sweatshirt on a deck in the middle of July. Shedding a prescribed melancholy right in front of everyone.

Months of not giving into it,
and then without warning on
full blast. So easy.

Moths not giving in, escaping
into wingfly like shadows.

Of reticence and maybe
October. October seems like
light years away.

A proximity so close you can
touch it.

Everyone's leaning into fist, hard, pressing on it and everyone's saying, Like a kamikaze takes flight! *and we're all sifting down to earth in these small significant bits, hamming it up trying to make ourselves larger, and we're laughing.*

If I had a father I'd say Dad.

But right smack in the middle, I hear someone say something about love and there are only fleeting attempts at annihilation.

I don't care how sentimental this all is.

Enter suitable caged beast,
fierce in blueness, blunting
here and there.

Dear god of gorgeous rooms, I
am yours.

What's missing? Leaf fallen.

Suddenly days go by with-
out words. The unconscious is
silent, too, always its muted
breath on the back of my neck.

– – –

I have been writing all my adult life about the irretrievable. Often the same image appears to me and finds language in the poem resembling the language in some other poem stroking the same wound. The image is of the hand outstretched, fingers pulsing—sometimes into blackness, a wandering depth; other times just short of the thing the hand needs to touch. The thing disappears. The hand begs and begs. I let the repetition occur across writings as layers, minute variations on a writing through time.

Your body is spinning in a room without furniture, white walls, you look out onto a stark beach, ocean with storm surges, waves too far back and too far in against shore. Caught at the window by the smallness of your own existence, you have the urge to wander but cannot. No feeling of a body present, instead inevitability.

– – –

Some Black Unknown

The body grieves in its heart chest—

An homage to Glenn Ligon's notation on the missing black women told
to support the protest by staying home

The *I* that is me lies forever in the mute mouth of the image.

Our water weight enters the room, bleeding gloriously from cunts, and
we are produced in the heel of cuff-mouth. Assertion as negation.

– – –

Once I wrote into being an imagined figure named Perpetuus, whose
name is Latin for "continuous, entire, universal." Perpetuus is neces-
sarily liberated from gender and without attachment to skin or color.
S/he is only reflection. S/he must be called to arrive and when she
arrives she alters the being of the one who called her forth and they
become what they have perceived in Perpetuus. What is the black
body but an aching tone? Perpetuus is untethered from the black
experience here on earth but has an outer core that is as dark as tree
in dead night. Refusal to adhere to ontology-as-fissure or rip in the
fictional coherence of culture ~~America~~ order. To build instead a sonic
register against any resistance to a white flag against which fists ~~male~~
aggress "a liberation."

– – –

To imagine a future as foretold now.
      To refute "it" am "s/he" —
—white-space-only adornment—décor.
      —peel back underneaths—
—hollowed be thy rage—thy cube—
Instead, slow cool into dead star,
      then nothing—

What speech do we have when we are crawling around on your
kitchen floor?

– – –

What is *life* against the quantifying of power? The partitioning of dearth? To excise *life* from the relations of power. The hand reaches out to grasp the lost object but it is not there; instead ghost space; instead hand floating; emptiness, a ball of fine threat unwinding, a trail of it barely visible in fading sunlight. In order to grieve properly you must remember—even if remembering is a non-space, more like a feeling than an image. Some say writing is an act of remembering. What has been forever lost. The sensations lodged in teeth cracks and throat muscles. What is the gesture of the wail but the wail? Is there such a thing as mute subjectivity? Or do we become animal in the grief state? Beast?

- - -

Desire, or as I call it, "despite its knee-dropping urgency," can take the form of a fragrance. What do you do when someone dies who you wanted to die?

- - -

Counterband [tangentials]

In folds as if between life, in life as if outside of the border, in the bustle of some hotel room in the city you live in, under spell, under scratch of regular linens, lights to guide you, city fog. Excellent. Who cares about the weather? Only the grace of looking. And you see your own body, once elderly, once gated, as a swift leap. You are no longer crippled. You say, *take me to the ocean,* even though the ocean has a thin layer of plastic. The metaphor is: the head of my own history. The figure eight in air I make with my fingers when I'm nervous, or thinking.

The stranger does not allow for memory. What does it mean to decipher this fact? An empty space in one's own cupped hand. Because we go on living despite many things. A commoner, a person just exploring life, will simply travel westward for adventure. It's quiet inside here. Can turn the ear toward a wet breeze. And, they ask us to think about all the world, and we do, as Sontag notes, only for the time it takes to think about our own safety. I am a fish. Not pondering the hook. The stranger, as we know, is no longer mine. Just the particulars of him, heavy dungeon against which we count nickels. This sensation through which we experience not want, but a material made between bodies on a bed not touching, what can be accessed only because it cannot be reached.

Formulations that you can discover anywhere. In the Mayan ruins, you find a remnant: dust it off, take the sheath off, reveal it to the known world and say here is the world before. What do we know from this fragile dust, we ask? *We are a civilization who knows civilization.* The feeling itself comes from this ignorance. Call it a blind spot. Call it a shoe worn over whole magics. You wander into a space that smells of the love of your life sprinkling lavender on your chest. You inhale so deeply you have to spit. To love incessantly despite the reader's inability to extract anything at all from the remnant. We can already look back says the reader. The worn-down stone at your toe. The ate-up nachos from yesterday. They will say they are not from yesterday but it's true. They are. The nachos shat out in the toilet. The toilet barely flushing. And, how's a man to strut? How's a strut to cock-hand, walking oe'r the land of the free, the weeping feet. A mother lost, a singer dead. The words "we hope." The abstractions of strength and virtue. They have it in the song. We sang the song eerie she interrupted the song barely unable to hear it sung. The land. The brave. The destitute. I worry. But, no space for endings. We could bury ourselves here. Or not. Or not.

Operatic, the Book Escapes the Book

We think there is escape—

But there is no escape. The material is always the same. Yet, it is malleable. To mutate is to live.

Make them spread and open to you.

One falls past the lip of some black unknown—

    where time, they say, ends. Whereas for extending, whereas what you might call a leaking or a wandering. Incalculable lang, incalculable list—what's spun down the hole. No pulling or leaping up. Blackness, only the din of our existence. Wishing-rod defunct. Hear my voice without echo, always present. A stone in hand. A crown in laughter.

Water weights—

float their heavy unmoored silence—likenesses of our selves. In persistence. Not the water itself, but of the water. No restlessness can reach us. No buildings can hinder our movement. Or, cement air. I often feel it out there, winding its tentacles to beastly effect. What if heavy as the road is, we swam it? We are the origin of life and also the end of everything. There will be others who squat down in their own shit, but this is not our business.

To sing the blue song of longing—

its webbed feet along jungle floor. What of our mechanical arm, our off-melody? Purpose in the gathering, I know, dear self. It rains and we think, *God,* or we think, *Universe.* I say, *portent across the wind.* When wind is wrought, whole song fallen from its lip, some black unknown. What speech into hard god breath just as night park is godless? What of a silver cube in the mouth? *This* is our wandering.

Faith is hum—

      hum is rocking. Rocking is to preserve our black bodies in glass. To hum is to maintain the myth of wholeness. What will we find in heart-cave, pull back sea-rot, the already multiple, the metropolis? *Look what I am holding! Not desire, but infinite multiplicity, the mouth of existence.* On one side waters rise.

We untangle—

     de-strange

our map-pings.

We are remove,

     the warrior in
living outer space,

incandescent. Open scab
—legend—and find uncut

surface. No return.

Image, we—

we scar, they want. Is dampness under blanket. Is tear in seam of all objects. Silver-white technological landscape before us. Blackness, desert. Whiteness, nothing. All, a brutal fantasy. My arm moves. Is it my arm? Has the *I* been cut out of the scene? The scene goes on, without gravity, without Mammy echo. Whole farms sacrificed, but we in holography, bigger and stronger. Uncontainered, without reference, without anchor. No longer the secure state of belonging. Hatched figures hang in stuck air, charred, and *that loss*. We begin long after the poultice time. Nowhere for them to find us.

Whereas sunlight—

    whereas matter and motion. You persist in concave before folds, carve a small incision, feed the white mouth a canned beat. Da da da da da da da da. Where is our excess limb, our pungent chests filled so tightly with gun of longing?

This skin with—its erotics

        memorials of our desires erected in town squares. How graceful to be inside of indeterminacy, my love, hot core forms, gathering dust, all small wallpapered rooms forgotten. They are excommunicated from joy. Ocean floor filled with dead wings and tar. The slaves blink their slow eyes.

—When they call to us

from cataclysmic flash—
and they will.

We will say, *How beautiful
our emergence in flame!*—

There, the sea went—
There, the edifice of offenses—
Of lions, of defunct crypts—

We lift her slight articulation
onto our shoulders, wanting,
for reasons we do not yet understand,
to know what will happen to the artifacts.
Who will rescue the records of eras
older than myth? How do we travel them
into the future?

White landscape lends us one new breath.
Waters take a body out and bring another in.

To be cradled with such fierce gentleness—

For all the burned languages—

       for all the silken hair
       and grope in heat of—

For all the openings against wills,
       howls against lips
sewn tight, and rough cuts in hours
before dawn, the handprints
       left as pungent reminders

For all of it, wet and steeled

Our mercurial grammar
       and this *I*-cleave
The black in the black body,
       a tremor so tender.

Dear empty vessel,

     from end to end,
along a fire road, plagues, then
rationalities. How to say, *We remain
in tact, however fractured?*

     How to say, *Whereas once restrained,
once ensnarement, now, sand—*

Leave wreckage by the roadside.

Burn all decayed tissue.

Tightrope from which we emerge.

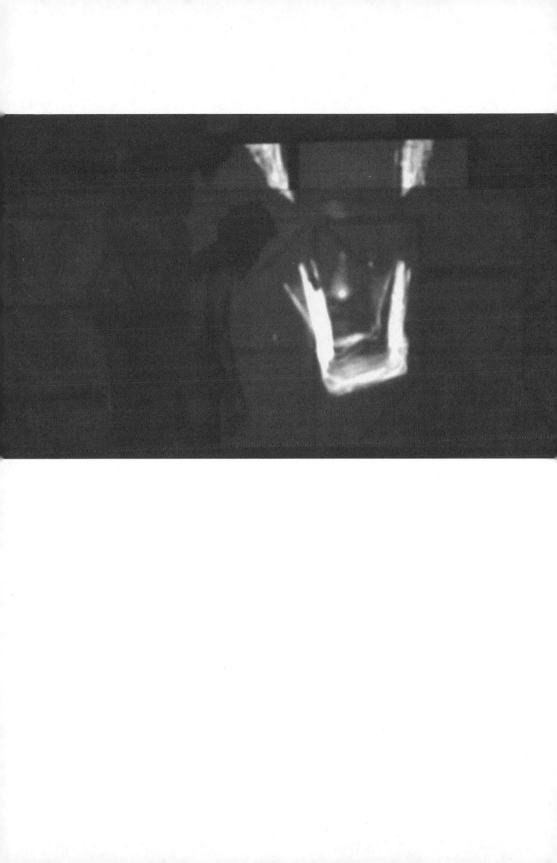

Acknowledgments

Extreme thanks to the artist Sienna Shields and the HOWDOYOUSAYYAMINAFRICAN? global artist's collective for inviting me to write the experimental libretto, *Good Stock on the Dimension Floor*, for the 2014 Whitney Biennial exhibition. The libretto became the bones for this collection, an investigation into the brutality of the raced condition and an embrace toward an AfroFuture outside of recognizable bodies, temporalities, and accessible dimensions. The Yam Collective and its members' wild imaginations pushed open the doors of the possible for this work. They taught me that there are no limits to the worlds we create and that we can manifest these worlds even, or especially, when repressive regimes take power.

I'm grateful as well to the following publications and individuals for publishing versions of this text: *BOMB*, *Hambone*, *Boston Review*, and *Poetry*. Some poems are also excerpted from the chapbook *Candy*, published by Brian Teare at Albion Books.

As always, I'm deeply grateful for my writing communities—the Black Took Collective (Ronaldo V. Wilson and Duriel E. Harris), Stephanie K. Hopkins and Kristin Dombek for forcing me to write when I am exhausted or feel *written out*, and Gala Mukomolova for her tireless conviction in this work. Thank you to Angie Cruz and Nelly Rosario for texting me strange late-night questions that led to the writing of the "Prologue," which until that moment had been plaguing me, resulting in clunky, tight prose. I could not have written this book without these interventions, just as I could not have written it without institutional support from the University of Pittsburgh and, also, the Lannan Foundation, which granted me a residency in Marfa—a truly altering experience that affected this work (and me) profoundly.

Love also alters me profoundly and makes it so that the conditions and experiences that undergird this book and my life's work don't annihilate. Thanks to my family, especially my chosen family, and my loves.

LITERATURE
is not the same thing as
PUBLISHING

Coffee House Press began as a small letterpress operation in 1972 and has grown into an internationally renowned nonprofit publisher of literary fiction, essay, poetry, and other work that doesn't fit neatly into genre categories.

Coffee House is both a publisher and an arts organization. Through our *Books in Action* program and publications, we've become inter-disciplinary collaborators and incubators for new work and audience experiences. Our vision for the future is one where a publisher is a catalyst and connector.

Funder Acknowledgments

Coffee House Press is an internationally renowned independent book publisher and arts nonprofit based in Minneapolis, MN; through its literary publications and *Books in Action* program, Coffee House acts as a catalyst and connector—between authors and readers, ideas and resources, creativity and community, inspiration and action.

Coffee House Press books are made possible through the generous support of grants and donations from corporations, state and federal grant programs, family foundations, and the many individuals who believe in the transformational power of literature. This activity is made possible by the voters of Minnesota through a Minnesota State Arts Board Operating Support grant, thanks to the legislative appropriation from the arts and cultural heritage fund. Coffee House also receives major operating support from the Amazon Literary Partnership, the Jerome Foundation, The McKnight Foundation, Target Foundation, and the National Endowment for the Arts (NEA). To find out more about how NEA grants impact individuals and communities, visit www.arts.gov.

Coffee House Press receives additional support from the Elmer L. & Eleanor J. Andersen Foundation; the David & Mary Anderson Family Foundation; the Buuck Family Foundation; the Dorsey & Whitney Foundation; Dorsey & Whitney LLP; the Fringe Foundation; the Knight Foundation; the Rehael Fund of the Minneapolis Foundation; the Matching Grant Program Fund of the Minneapolis Foundation; Mr. Pancks' Fund in memory of Graham Kimpton; the Schwab Charitable Fund; Schwegman, Lundberg & Woessner, P.A.; the US Bank Foundation; VSA Minnesota for the Metropolitan Regional Arts Council; and the Woessner Freeman Family Foundation in honor of Allan Kornblum.

The Publisher's Circle of Coffee House Press

Publisher's Circle members make significant contributions to Coffee House Press's annual giving campaign. Understanding that a strong financial base is necessary for the press to meet the challenges and opportunities that arise each year, this group plays a crucial part in the success of Coffee House's mission.

Recent Publisher's Circle members include many anonymous donors, Mr. & Mrs. Rand L. Alexander, Suzanne Allen, Patricia A. Beithon, Bill Berkson & Connie Lewallen, the E. Thomas Binger & Rebecca Rand Fund of the Minneapolis Foundation, Robert & Gail Buuck, Claire Casey, Louise Copeland, Jane Dalrymple-Hollo, Ruth Stricker Dayton, Jennifer Kwon Dobbs & Stefan Liess, Mary Ebert & Paul Stembler, Chris Fischbach & Katie Dublinski, Kaywin Feldman & Jim Lutz, Sally French, Jocelyn Hale & Glenn Miller, the Rehael Fund-Roger Hale/Nor Hall of the Minneapolis Foundation, Randy Hartten & Ron Lotz, Jeffrey Hom, Carl & Heidi Horsch, Amy L. Hubbard & Geoffrey J. Kehoe Fund, Kenneth Kahn & Susan Dicker, Stephen & Isabel Keating, Kenneth Koch Literary Estate, Allan & Cinda Kornblum, Leslie Larson Maheras, Lenfestey Family Foundation, Sarah Lutman & Rob Rudolph, the Carol & Aaron Mack Charitable Fund of the Minneapolis Foundation, George & Olga Mack, Joshua Mack, Gillian McCain, Mary & Malcolm McDermid, Sjur Midness & Briar Andresen, Maureen Millea Smith & Daniel Smith, Peter Nelson & Jennifer Swenson, Marc Porter & James Hennessy, Enrique Olivarez, Jr. & Jennifer Komar, Robin Preble, Jeffrey Scherer, Jeffrey Sugerman & Sarah Schultz, Alexis Scott, Nan G. & Stephen C. Swid, Patricia Tilton, Stu Wilson & Melissa Barker, Warren D. Woessner & Iris C. Freeman, Margaret Wurtele, Joanne Von Blon, and Wayne P. Zink & Christopher Schout.

For more information about the Publisher's Circle and other ways to support Coffee House Press books, authors, and activities, please visit www.coffeehousepress.org/support or contact us at info@coffeehousepress.org.

Dawn Lundy Martin is a poet, essayist, and conceptual-video artist. She is the author of three books of poems and three chapbooks, including, most recently, *Life in a Box is a Pretty Life* (Nightboat Books 2015), which won the Lambda Literary Award for Lesbian Poetry. Her nonfiction can be found in the *New Yorker, Harper's,* and other magazines. Martin is an associate professor of English in the writing program at the University of Pittsburgh.

Good Stock Strange Blood was designed by
Bookmobile Design and Digital Publisher Services.
Text is set in Adobe Caslon Pro.